EXPLORE NASHVILLE'S MUSIC VALLEY

DATES IN THE STATES

A COUPLE TRAVELING THE UNITED
STATES ON A BUDGET

Mystery Date
Nashville, TN

By Dates in the States

![Nashville Palace and Legends of Country Music Museum street scene]

SPONSOR

THIS MYSTERY DATE IS SPONSORED BY:

Legends of Country Music Museum

Proudly family-owned and operated for over 45 years, Legends of Country Music Museum is the perfect stop for any fan of classic country. From furniture from Willie Nelson's studio to the Bocephus truck and memorabilia from 35+ country legends, their friendly and knowledgeable staff will make your visit unforgettable.

As a Partner & Seller of the Music Valley Mystery Date Book, Legends of Country Music Museum is not only featured in this book, but also serves as an official pickup point. Stop by, explore, and take home a memory of your Music Valley adventure!

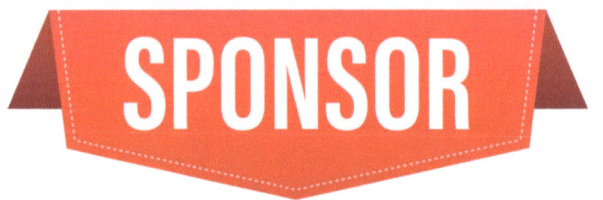

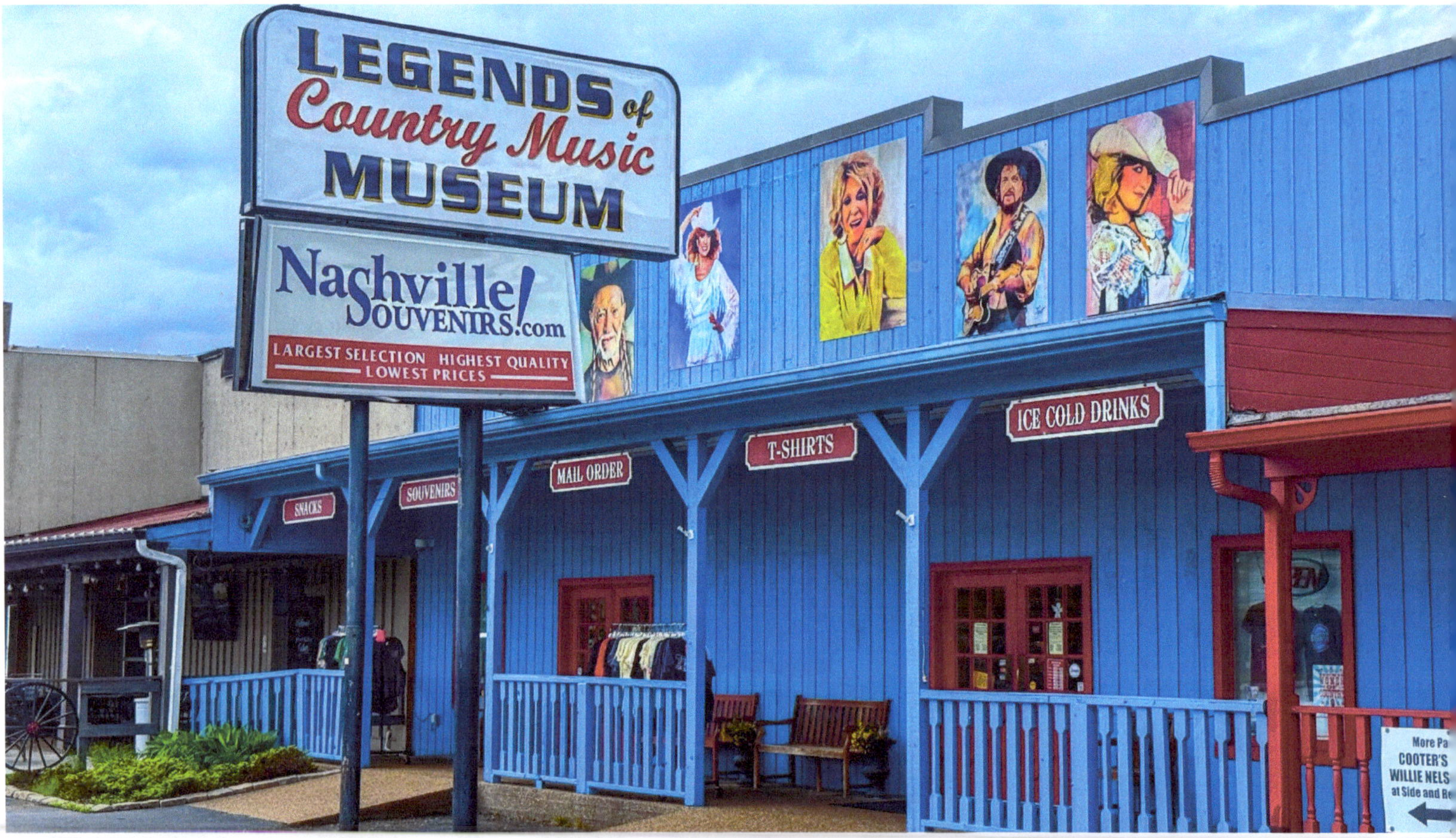

"Our passion is travel, and we want to share our adventures to inspire others to explore the world with their loved ones. Dare to live beyond the box."

Dates in the States

Introduction

Hey there! We're Crystal and Shane, the duo behind Dates in the States, where we share our love for discovering unique adventures, unforgettable moments, and hidden gems across the U.S. Whether you're searching for a fun date idea, a new place to explore, or just a little inspiration, we've got you covered!

Our Mystery Date Books are designed to help couples (and adventurous friends!) shake up their routine and experience the best local spots in a fun, intentional way. Inside, you'll find a curated collection of date ideas. Each one meant to be completed over the course of a single day in a specific neighborhood. All of which are a surprise until you flip the page!

It's like a little challenge to break out of your comfort zone, support local, and make memories that stick. We hope this book helps you laugh more, explore more, and connect more, with each other and with your city. Let the mystery begin!

Here's What To Expect:

In this Mystery Date Book, we're taking you to Nashville's vibrant Music Valley. A lively area bursting with rich country music history, unique shops, and unforgettable dining experiences.

Here's what to expect for your day ahead:

Start your morning with a warm cup of coffee at a cozy local café, then browse charming vintage treasures at an antique store. Next, dive into the heart of country music with visits to the local museums. For lunch, enjoy a one-of-a-kind dining experience inside the Mall, followed by some leisurely shopping and exploring. Cap off your day with a peaceful stroll through the breathtaking botanical gardens and finish with a delicious dinner at a historical venue.

Soak in the spirit of Music Valley. Let's dive in!

Start

Nashville Coffees

2416 Music Valley Dr #143
Nashville, TN 37214

Start your Music Valley date the perfect way, with a cozy stop at Nashville Coffees. This charming café is a cool, vibey spot in this neighborhood. Walk in and you might catch some live music setting the perfect mood. The pistachio white mocha is a standout - rich, creamy, and delicious. Plus, they offer plenty of sugar-free syrup options, so you can customize your drink just how you like it. Nashville Coffees isn't just about great coffee; it's about an atmosphere that makes your morning feel special.

Second Stop

Music Valley Antiques & Marketplace

2416 Music Valley Dr #126

Nashville, TN 37214

One of our favorite things to do in every city is exploring local antique and thrift stores, which is why we had to include Music Valley Antiques & Marketplace.

While exploring, see if you can find one item that sparks a story—maybe a vintage record, an old postcard, or a quirky knick-knack. Share with your date what you imagine its history might be, or pick something small to take home as a memory of your Music Valley adventure. Tip: Their days and hours are limited, so be sure to check ahead to make sure it fits perfectly into your date plans!

Third Stop
Legends of Country Music Museum

2613A McGavock Pk
Nashville, TN 37214

Once known as the Willie Nelson Museum, the Legends of Country Music Museum got a fresh new chapter in early 2025 when longtime employee Jenny bought it out. Jenny is amazing - passionate and knowledgeable, she'll happily answer any questions you have about the classic country greats.

Inside, you'll find iconic memorabilia like furniture from Willie Nelson's studio, the famous Bocephus truck (check out the beer tubes on the driver's seat - that's how he drank on the road!), and even the original Braille Playboy.

This museum showcases artifacts from 35+ classic country legends. The staff is incredibly friendly, and the souvenir shop offers some of the best deals on Nashville-themed merchandise around. If you love country music, this spot is an absolute must-visit.

Fourth Stop

Cooter's Nashville

2613B McGavock Pk
Nashville, TN 37214

Right next door to the Legends of Country Music Museum is Cooter's Nashville, a must-see for any Dukes of Hazzard fan. Step inside and you'll find a treasure trove of Dukes memorabilia, from hitch covers to valve covers, all proudly painted bright orange with the iconic "01", the signature look of the General Lee car.

Whether you're a longtime fan or just curious, this spot is packed with fun exhibits, collectibles, and nostalgic pieces that celebrate the legendary TV show. It's a playful, laid-back stop that adds a bit of down-home charm and excitement to your Music Valley adventure. Be sure to swing by and grab a souvenir or two!

Fifth Stop

Opry Mills Mall

433 Opry Mills Dr
Nashville, TN 37214

By now, you might be feeling hungry. Perfect timing to head over to Opry Mills Mall. This bustling shopping destination has plenty to explore, but our favorite spot to refuel is the Aquarium Restaurant.

Enjoy a unique dining experience surrounded by a massive fish tank, where fresh seafood and tasty dishes come with a side of mesmerizing aquatic views. It's the perfect place to relax, eat, and soak up some cool vibes before you continue your Music Valley adventure.

After lunch, feel free to walk the mall and stop in even more souvenir shops (you can never have too many, right?). And have some fun at the Madame Tussauds Nashville wax museum if time and budget allows.

Sixth Stop
Gaylord Opryland Resort
2800 Opryland Dr
Nashville, TN 37214

Okay, full disclosure - the real reason we wanted you to head to Opry Mills Mall isn't just for shopping or lunch (though those are great too!). It's because the mall has free parking, making it the perfect spot to leave your car while you walk over to the Gaylord Opryland Resort.

Yes, we know it sounds a little weird to include a resort as a date stop. But trust us, you won't regret it. The resort is home to stunning indoor botanical gardens that are absolutely magical. Honestly, you could spend all day wandering these beautiful, lush spaces filled with waterfalls, exotic plants, and charming pathways. It's a peaceful, romantic oasis right in the middle of Music Valley.

So park free, take a leisurely walk, and get ready to be amazed!
If it's too far to walk, you may park at the resort for a fee.

Final Stop

The Nashville Palace

2611 McGavock Pk
Nashville, TN 37214

Ok, we know we've made you do A LOT of walking and exploring, but this is your last stop. You've made it. And trust us - it's worth it.

End your perfect Music Valley day with dinner at The Nashville Palace - a true Nashville classic. Enjoy a hearty meal while soaking up the lively atmosphere, then settle in for a show featuring some of the best live country music around. Whether you're tapping your toes to a band or just enjoying the vibe, The Palace offers an unforgettable finale to your day. It's the perfect mix of great food, great music, and great company.

Add Your Photos

Keepsakes

Thank you for joining us on this mystery date adventure! We hope you've enjoyed the delightful experiences and memorable moments we've crafted just for you in Nashville's Music Valley.

But the adventure doesn't stop here! Keep exploring exciting mystery dates in other cities and uncover new experiences across the U.S. by visiting our website, DatesintheStates.com. There, you can purchase both physical copies and digital downloads of our mystery date books.

Plus, don't miss out on our Mystery Date Book Club, where you can receive a brand-new mystery date book every month!
Tag us in your date photos on social media! @datesinthestates

About the Creators

Crystal, the writer and creator, is a storyteller at heart. When she's not uncovering hidden gems for the next date night idea, she runs her own digital marketing company, helping small businesses improve their content marketing, increase visibility in their communities, and streamline their online presence.
Visit: crystalstatskey.com

Shane, her husband and partner in adventure, is a dedicated personal trainer and the owner of Beekstar Fitness in Irondequoit, NY. He specializes in working with clients who have limited mobility, helping them build muscle and focus on pain areas so they can regain strength and confidence in their daily lives.
Visit: beekstarfitness.com

Crystal and Shane have explored every U.S. state except Alaska (coming soon!) and are now visiting countries in alphabetical order. Whether road-tripping or curating Mystery Date experiences, they're always chasing their next adventure.

Local Love

A few local gems in Music Valley worth exploring on your next date.

THE CATIO CAT LOUNGE
ADORABLE CAT CAFE
2416 MUSIC VALLEY DR SUITE 119, NASHVILLE, TN 37214

CANEY FORK RIVER VALLEY GRILLE
RESTAURANT W/SOUTHERN FOOD & LAID BACK VIBES
2400 MUSIC VALLEY DR, NASHVILLE, TN 37214

GRAND OLE OPRY
HISTORICAL MUSIC VENUE
600 OPRY MILLS DR, NASHVILLE, TN 37214

Want to see your business here? See the next page for details on how to join!

Want to be featured?

MYSTERY DATE BOOK PACKAGES

Are you a small business looking to reach new customers? Feature your business in our next Mystery Date Book! Choose from our partnership packages below to connect with couples seeking unique experiences and exclusive deals.

Package One

LOCAL LOVE LISTING

A quick shoutout to show you're part of the neighborhood vibe.

Listed in the "Local Love" section of your designated neighborhood date book

Includes business name, address, and social link

Optional: Offer a small promo (e.g., 10% off for book holders)

1 social media shout-out when the book launches

$45

Package Two

FEATURE STOP

You're not just a business— you're part of the experience.

Marked as a "Must-Stop" on a Mystery Date

Full-page feature in the book with your story, offerings and photo

Includes 1 social media feature — a dedicated post and story highlighting your business

Note: To ensure each feature is genuine and experience-based, we require a hosted visit prior to inclusion.

$95

Package Three

PARTNER & SELLER

Be the spot and the source.

Everything in Tier 2

PLUS: Option to sell the Mystery Date Books at your location

Includes a bulk purchase of 10 books (yours to price + sell)

Keep 100% of the profits from in-store sales

Bonus: Have a featured "sponsored by" page and listed as an official pickup location in our promotions

$250

Prices are subject to change

Feel free to reach us at any time by sending us an email to say hi and to learn more! We look forward to hearing from you.

| www.datesinthestates.com | datesinthestatesblog@gmail.com |

Sponsors & Affiliates

Our sponsors and affiliates help make our adventures possible! Explore the amazing brands and businesses that support our community.

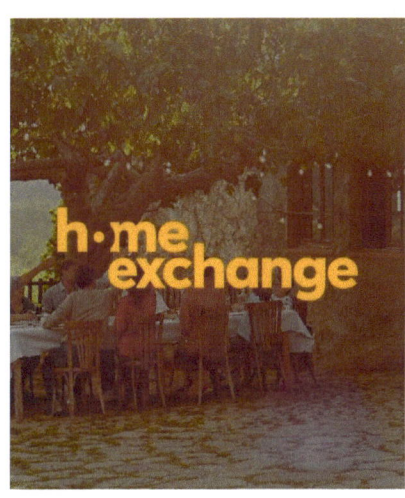

Wanderful

Wanderful is a global community for women who love to travel. Connect, explore, and join a local hub near you!

Join our Book Club!

Join our Mystery Date Book Club and be part of a travel-inspired community, discovering unique local adventures together!

HomeExchange

HomeExchange lets you swap homes with travelers worldwide for authentic, affordable stays. Join today and travel differently!

Shop our books at a store near you!

Little Button Craft
658 South Ave.
Rochester, NY 14620

The Pawsitive Cat Cafe
120 East Ave. Ste 100
Rochester, NY 14604

Yesterday's Muse Books
32 West Main St.
Webster, NY 14580

Nashville Souvenirs
2613 McGavock Pk,
Nashville, TN 37214

usic Valley Antiques
416 Music Valley Dr.
Nashville, TN 37214

Barnes & Noble
1 Walden Galleria g113,
Buffalo, NY 14225

Abundance Food Co-op
571 South Ave,
Rochester, NY 14620

Union Tavern
4565 Culver Rd,
Irondequoit, NY 14622

DATES IN THE STATES

A COUPLE TRAVELING THE UNITED
STATES ON A BUDGET

Contact Us

🌐

datesinthestates.com

✉

datesinthestatesblog@gmail.com

📍

Based in Rochester, NY

CONNECT WITH US ON SOCIAL!
@DATESINTHESTATES

www.ingramcontent.com/pod-product-compliance
Lightning Source LLC
Chambersburg PA
CBHW041621120626
46551CB00003B/534